Nyansa Classical Community Teacher's Guide
Copyright © 2025 by Nyansa Classical Community

Published in the United States by Nyansa Classical Community
2416 S. Derbigny St.
New Orleans, LA 70125
nyansaclassicalcommunity.org

To order additional materials, please go to www.nyansaclassicalcommunity.org

ISBN 978-1-967443-04-8 (paperback)
ISBN 978-1-967443-05-5 (eBook)

Cover design by Laura Duffy
Book design by Sarah Scudder
Illustrations by Josslyn Littles
Content developed by Dr. Angel Adams Parham and Interns from Nyansa Classical Community

Printed in the United States of America

Resources

Additional online training videos and sample lesson videos are available with the purchase of our Nyansa Year One Training Guide.

To request these training and sample videos, please email us at nyansa.assistant@gmail.com.

Credit

Originally developed by Dr. Angel Adams Parham, Co-Founder and Executive Director of Nyansa Classical Community

Design and Formatting by Sarah Scudder, Assistant Director of Nyansa Classical Community

Lessons Written by Sara Smith

Illustrations by Josslyn Littles

Acknowledgements

Thank you to the following organization for their support and funding:

Please Note: *This guide provides details for <u>one week of programming,</u> broken down into Day 1 through Day 4. Each week features a different virtue explored through related classical literature, Bible stories, art, and Aesop fables. Typically, each day is organized as follows:*

1. *Opening time with all the children together.*

2. *Break into three smaller groups based on age. The children rotate from one group to another, spending 30-40 minutes in each group. The groups are: Literature, Bible, Art, and Latin (using Aesop fables).*

Although the guide is written with this structure in mind, please feel free to adapt as much or as little as works best for your context, whether in a large group or small homeschool. Enjoy!

Opening Time:

The guidelines provide suggestions for how to structure your opening time. Adapt these as makes sense for your context. The opening time generally follows the same routine for every meeting. If you are homeschooling, then the lessons can be adapted to working with your own children, or working with a larger group of children in a co-op.

- As the children enter the room, encourage them to sit quietly, ready to begin. As you see a child who is sitting quietly at attention, call their name, affirm that they are "ready" and give them two "gems". Gems can later be exchanged for prizes, usually once a month. Continue to acknowledge each child as he/she is ready and award them gems.

- Open in prayer.

- Make any announcements. This is also a good time to do introductions of new children or staff.

- Hand out snack. (If this is an appropriate time for snack.) Encourage good table manners during this time.

- Once snack is complete, have the children gather into three groups, based on age or affinity. It is best that these groups be set so that children know from day to day which group they are in. The children will circulate between four activities: literature, Bible, art, and Latin.

- If each activity meets in a different room, dismiss them to go to the appropriate room or space with their group.

- The children will rotate between room, dismiss them to go to the appropriate room or space with their group.

- The children will rotate between the four different activities, spending about 30-40 minutes in each. Thus, the entire period will be 1.5 to 2 hours.

Please note: Each unit is designed to be carried out over the course of four days. There are twenty units in total, so twenty weeks of material. This might be divided into ten weeks in the fall and ten weeks in the spring. Activities for unit one on the virtue of love are detailed below.

LITERATURE GROUP WEEK 1 - DEMETER

Please note that it is quite possible you will not get through all of the activities described for a given day's session. **That's okay! There is no rush!** Whatever is not done in one session can be taken up or continued the next time you meet. We lean toward providing lots of options for a meeting because what engages the children's attention one day may not engage it another day. Also, because children cycle through each of the three activities in each meeting day, you will be doing the same activity with three different groups of children. In that case, you may find that one group really gets into a certain activity while another group does not. Having multiple methods of entry into the material provides flexibility for you as an instructor to use, adapt, and tailor as works best for you and the children on any given day.

DAY ONE -

LESSON 1: DEMETER - GREEK GODDESS OF THE EARTH

DISCUSS: Today we will be discussing **love** and **hate**. Discuss what each means. Create a new memory card for each term with its meaning and its opposite on the back of the card. These can be used for memory matching games once there are enough of them. Identify themes that go with the story and write terms and definitions on flash cards.

Focus Virtue: Love is caring for a person or thing very much and wishing good towards them.

Vice: Hate is disliking a person or thing very much and wishing harm towards them.

READ: Read through the story of Demeter and Persephone (Greek Gods #1). Encourage narration activities as students listen (drawing, writing, etc.) During a narration activity the instructor reads a story and afterward the children tell the story back. **The process helps them to deepen their listening, comprehension, and presentation skills.** This telling or narrating back can be done verbally, with drawings, acting the story out, etc. Each student should have a narration notebook or *Nyansa Year One Literature Workbook* that can be used for drawing and writing. (See the Appendix for more on the kinds of notebooks to use for this exercise and for the dictation exercise that will be described for Day 2.) Have your student write and/or draw a narration of the story in the Narration section of their workbook or in their narration notebook. Have students share their narration activity as a way of telling back the story.

DEMETER AND PERSEPHONE

One of the Greek's favorite goddesses was Demeter, the goddess of the earth and of the harvest. In our own day, you may have heard people use the term "Mother Earth," and the Greeks thought of Demeter in that way- she was kind, motherly person, and the Greeks prayed to her in hopes of getting a good harvest out of the ground. Demeter was also one of Zeus' sisters, and therefore one of the more important and powerful goddesses. The Greeks believed that Demeter caused crops to grow, trees to bud, and flowers to blossom. They particularly loved to draw Demeter on vases. In these drawings, she often wears a crown and has sheaves of wheat or flowers in her hands. This story gives the Greeks' explanation for why plants only grow for three quarters of the year because of Demeter's love for her daughter Persephone.

Hades, the grim god of the dead, wanted a wife, but no one wanted to live with him in Erebos, his dark and cold land. So Hades asked Zeus for a wife, and Zeus promised him the hand of beautiful Persephone, Demeter's graceful daughter. Persephone loved flowers more than anything else, and she delighted to dance in the sun next to her kind mother. Zeus knew that Persephone would never go with Hades willingly, so he tricked the young woman into leaving her mother's side by creating a most marvelous flower in a meadow far away.

Persephone was delighted by the gorgeous flower, but when she reached down to pick it, the ground opened up and Hades emerged with a chariot and four black horses! Hades picked up Persephone, dropped her into his chariot, and plunged back into the earth. With a scream from Persephone, the ground closed back up behind them, leaving no trace of the Demeter's sun-loving daughter. Before long, Demeter realized Persephone was missing.

Demeter loved her daughter more than anything else, and for nine days she walked all over the earth looking for her beloved child. In all that time, she did not eat, drink, or bathe. Eventually, the other gods took pity on her and Helios, the sun god, confessed that he had seen Hades steal her daughter. Thinking of her beautiful sun-loving daughter as a prisoner in that cold and dreary world with stern Hades made Demeter weep. She was so sad that she sat huddled in a heap and could not be comforted. When she realized Zeus was behind it all, she refused to set foot on Mount Olympus again until she had her daughter back. She also refused to allow another seed to sprout from the ground until Hades returned Persephone.

Up on his lofty throne, shining Zeus realized the situation was getting desperate. If no crops grew upon the earth, all the people would die, and there would be no one to worship the gods! So he sent the messenger god, Hermes, down to dark Erebos to bring back Persephone.

"But," warned Zeus sternly, "if she has eaten any food from the underworld, she will have to remain there." Hermes sped away to Erebos on his winged sandals.

Before the dark throne, Hermes said, "Oh lord Hades, god of death and spirits, Zeus orders you to return the lovely Persephone, for if you fail, Demeter will cause no seed to grow out of the ground and all of mankind will die."

Hades reluctantly agreed, but he pulled Persephone aside to talk with her first. He said, "Oh my lovely bride, please do not think harshly of me, for I would have been a good and gentle husband to you, and made you my queen of all the underworld. And now, take as a small gift from me, three pomegranate seeds to eat on your journey back to the land of the living."

And with that he kissed her and returned her to Hermes. Persephone smiled a gentle smile - she was so happy to return to her loving mother, and yet Hades had surprised her with his gentleness and kindness. She happily ate the seed and skipped behind Hermes all the way back to the sunlit land above.

Up to Demeter's fair temple they sped. When Demeter saw Persephone, her heart leaped. Demeter ran to Persephone and wrapped her in her arms. Suddenly she felt afraid; what if something had gone wrong?

"My dearest daughter," said Demeter all of a sudden, "Did you eat anything down in the underworld? Please tell me at once!"

"Not at first, Mother, but Hades gave me three pomegranate seeds as I was leaving and I ate it. Was that wrong?" Persephone looked anxiously up at her mother.

Demeter clung to her daughter, unwilling to give her back. But wise Zeus proposed a compromise: Persephone would spend three months every year with Hades, but the rest of the year she could live on the good green earth with her mother if Demeter agreed to make the crops grown again. Joyfully, both of them agreed. Demeter ran over the whole earth. Persephone at her side. As they ran, crops sprouted, trees budded, and flowers pushed through the tender soil all over the earth. And so, the Greeks believed that winter came because Demeter sat and mourned for her daughter for three months every year, but when Persephone returned, spring came again and life grew everywhere upon the earth because of Demeter's love and joy.

Cultural Note: Sometimes, the Greeks drew Demeter carrying a cornucopia. The word "cornucopia" means "horn of plenty." You may have seen a picture of one around Thanksgiving time - it looks like a horn-shaped basket full of crops like pumpkins, apples, wheat, and so on. Even today, although Americans do no worship Demeter, we use a cornucopia to represent a harvest celebration.

- After narration activities are completed, have children practice saying the memory sentence for the Demeter story.

- Discuss children's responses to the discussion questions provided with the story and/or create your own discussion questions.

DISCUSS:

Discuss the following questions.

1. Who demonstrated love in this story? Do you see any hate in the story?

2. Why did Hades give Persephone the pomegranate seeds to eat? Was that the loving thing to do?

3. Why did Zeus agree to give Persephone back to Demeter? Do you think the compromise was fair?

4. Have you ever lost someone or something you loved very much?

MEMORY:

Memorize the sentence below.

Demeter loved Persephone and got her back from Hades.

FOLLOW-UP ACTIVITIES:

1. DRESS UP

Have the children act out the story. **Keeping a dress-up box** with items that go with the story allows the children to act the story out with relevant props. Here are some suggested dress-up items for the Demeter story.

- flowers
- Basket of produce
- Pomegranate seed
- Black robe (Hades)
- Blue robe (Demeter)

- Crown (Demeter)
- Sandals (Hermes)
- Tiara (Persephone)
- Thunder bolt (Zeus)

2. BRAINSTORM

Print out the full-page image of Demeter which is included in the lesson. Tape or glue this image to a large piece of planning paper. You will work with the children to brainstorm descriptive words that go along with the story of Demeter. These words will become a word bank that the children will use to write poetry, narrative summaries, etc. When writing poetry, the haiku poetry form is ideal as it is simple and allows for reinforcing the idea of syllables for young children.

Here below are some words that work for the main characters and places mentioned in the story. Feel free to let the kids come up with their own words, but if they're having trouble, you can get things going by suggesting some on the lists below. Write the main persons, places and things from the story up on white board or paper with space beneath them. Brainstorm descriptive words to go under each or have descriptive words written in advance on stickies for younger kids. In the case of younger children, call out each term and ask for a student volunteer to put each term under the person, place or thing that it describes. Keep this for the next session.

Students can record these words and ideas in the Brainstorm section of the Nyansa Year One Literature Workbook.

PEOPLE

- Demeter - goddess of the earth, kind, loving, mature, maternal, motherly, tender

- Persephone - sun-loving, young, sweet, beautiful, stolen, sad, graceful

- Hades - stern, dark, cold, selfish, thief, trickster

- Zeus - lofty, king of the gods, promise-maker, regretful, worried

- Hermes - messenger, quick, speedy

- Helios - god of the sun, truthful, compassionate

PLACES

- Earth - beautiful, sunny, grassy, covered with flowers, delightful, full of life

- Erebos - dark, gloomy, cold, land of the dead

DAY TWO -

DISCUSS:

1. Review the concepts "love" and "hate". Use the memory cards created for the previous session.

2. Review the memory sentences presented in the previous session.

3. Use the corresponding copywork page in Nyansa Year One Literature Workbook to copy the memory sentence.

FOLLOW-UP ACTIVITIES:

1. DICTATION

Introduce the dictation activity. Dictation is an activity that helps students to strengthen their skills of learning, writing, and spelling. For children who are able to write, the activity consists in the instructor slowly reading the dictation text as the student attempt to write exactly what is being said, including punctuation.

Note: Say the sentence only once. This will help students to give attention to the sentence. See what they can write after hearing the sentence only one time. After the student writes as much of the sentence as they can remember, you can then fill in the missing words.

We divide the dictation sentences into three increasing levels of difficulty: pre-k and kindergarten, early elementary, and later elementary. For pre-k and kindergarten, rather than writing out the sentence, children are given a dictation sheet which simply has a choice of letters for four items. The instructor reads the word and students circle or underline the letter choice which shows the sound the word starts with.

For children who can write and spell, after reading the sentence once, you can then repeat the sentence or sentences a few times, speaking slowly and clearly to give them plenty of time to get it down as accurately as possible.

Dictation as a Team Game

To make this into a game, divide the children into teams. They will do their dictation exercises separately at first, but each person on the team who gets the dictation correct will get two points. Team members who make mistakes will get one point for their efforts. Before the instructor writes the correct sentence on the board, consider allowing team members to review each other's word and discuss corrections. This way, the children can help each other and each team maximize their number of points.

EXAMPLE:

Pre-K and Kindergarten

The pre-k exercises are provided on a worksheet as seen in the picture provided.

- Demeter - begins with N, D, A, or P

- Winter - begins with N, O, W, or K

- Hades - beings with H, R, Q, or T

Student Dictation Sheet for Pre-K and Kindergarten

1. N D A P

2. N O W K

3. H R Q T

4. U K S E

Elementary Level

Early and later elementary students should complete their dictation exercises in their individual notebooks or in the dictation section in their Nyansa Year One Literature Workbook. See the Appendix for more on the kind of notebooks to use.

Early Elementary

- Demeter was sad that Hades took her girl.

- Demeter was sad that Hades stole Persephone to be his wife.

(For this more complex version of the sentence, it makes sense to write on the board the spelling for uncommon names like Demeter, Hades, and Persephone.)

Later Elementary

- Demeter was so sad to lose Persephone that she stopped helping the crops to grow. Zeus made Hades give Persephone back to Demeter for most of the year.

2.   CREATIVE WRITING

Once dictation is done, if there's still time left, go back to the brainstorming page with the word bank and complete that if there's still more to be done. If it was completed last session, then introduce the haiku form and show them the sample haiku based on some of the words from the brainstorming exercise. Here's an example from words provided in this guide:

Note: Persephone is pronounced (pur-se-fa-nee)

Demeter is sad (5 syllables)

Hades, dark, selfish trickster (7 syllables)

Steals Persephone (5 syllables)

Each child's poetry should be written into their individual narration notebook or in the poem section of Nyansa Year One Literature Workbook. If the child is too young to write, they can dictate to an adult who writes for them. Compile these poems into a single program notebook, careful to label each poem with the correct child's name. At the end of the year, these can be bound into a poetry book and duplicated so that each family has a copy. This end-of-year publication may also include children's artwork, narrative summaries, reflections, etc. It's a wonderful memory book and provides lots of pride for both children and parents to see what their children have produced. This book will also act as a gathering of memories that help students to remember all that they have learned about this year.

3.   CLOSING GAMES

See Appendix. Opportunity for more gems (e.g. number knockout; card matching game based on story, etc.).

Note: Groups in the past have awarded students with toy gems. These can be earned for games, completed work, etc. Students can then trade the gems in for prizes at the end of a period of time.

DAY THREE -

DISCUSS - Review the concepts love and hate. Use the memory cards created for the previous session. Ask the students to recall the memory sentence for this story.

MEMORIZE - Introduce the poem below which students can memorize as a way of remembering the key aspects of the story. The text can be recited as poetry; or it can be rapped or sung if the students would like to add melody or beats.

POEM: THE GODDESS DEMETER

A beautiful goddess of heaven and rebirth,
Demeter was known to be a mother to the Earth,
Flowers bloomed from her beauty and love,
She was a powerful goddess in the sky above.

Her daughter Persephone loved nature and the sun,
Through the meadows and fields she was delighted to run.
Until one day Hades wanted a wife,
He begged Zeus to give him part of her life.

Persephone was doomed to the underworld,
Demeter had lost her lovely little girl,
She cried and cried for three months straight,
Because Persephone was doomed to a gloomy fate.
From hades Pomegranate were three berries she ate.

And now winter lasts three full months long,
When Demeter cries, not a smile nor song.
The other nine months are filled with cheer,
Because spring, summer, and Persephone is here!

CREATIVE WRITING

Work with the children on their own original poetry based on the story of Demeter. Use the word bank created earlier in the week.

Have older children work on writing their own version of the Demeter story with illustrations. This is best done in their individual notebook lined on one side and blank on the other or students can use the poetry section in Nyansa Year One Literature Workbook. See Appendix for photos of this kind of notebook with sample student writing and illustrations.

Close out the story of Demeter by inviting students to present the poetry, pictures, and/or other writing they have done this week.

CLOSING GAMES

See Appendix. Opportunity for more gems (i.e. number knockout, card matching game based on story, etc.).

DAY FOUR -

Learning Through Art

See Learning Through Art Week 1 for instructions.

Artist: Jacob Lawrence. Title: Migration Series Panel 1 - "During World War I there was a great migration north by southern African Americans"
Date: 1940-41 Size: 12 x 18in. Materials: Casein tempera on hardboard. Where the artwork is located now: The Phillips Collection, Washington, D.C.

LEARNING THROUGH ART

Week One - Jacob Lawrence, Migration Series Panel 1

"During World War I there was a great migration north by southern African Americans."

JACOB LAWRENCE, MIGRATION SERIES

Day 4 of each week is devoted to learning through art. The weekly theme continues to be explored through contemplation and hands-on production of artwork.

This semester, we will be learning about African American art and history by studying and emulating panels from Jacob Lawrence's Migration Series (next semester the focus will be on Diego Rivera's mural along with Mexican and Mexican-American history and culture.) Each week we will do a picture study of one of the panels and children will imitate the panel using various media.

The virtue/vice focus for the week will be used to discuss what is going on in the painting: **Love and Hate: Jacob Lawrence Panel 1 of Migration Series.** Read the summary below, which explains the subject matter of Lawrence's Migration Series.

OBSERVE:

Tell students that we will study another panel of Jacob Lawrence's Migration Series. This is Panel 1. Print out a full-page copy of the panel for the students. Give them two minutes to observe the painting quietly for themselves. Tell them that the goal is for them to remember it so well that they can picture it in their minds eyes closed.

DISCUSS:

When the two minutes are over, ask the students to turn their copies of the painting over, picture side down. Ask them what they saw in the painting. Get them to be as descriptive as possible. Can they remember the objects/people? What did it look like was happening? What were the colors? Shapes? Sizes? Placement of elements in the picture? What were the people doing? How did they look—happy, sad, tired, bored, angry? For instance, you see men and women, children, even the outline of a baby. Part of what we are looking for in a picture study activity is to train the children to pay close attention to what they are seeing and to narrate what they are seeing and how it helps to convey mood, tone, ideas, etc. Once the painting has been throughly described, turn the picture back over and discuss anything that was missed or described incorrectly.

Consider the themes we're focusing on this week: Love and Hate. Ask the following discussion questions or use questions of your own as appropriate for the students and context:

1. How might people be motivated by love to move across the country to a place they don't know?

2. How might hate or some other negative experience push a person to leave their home to go somewhere else?

CREATE:

Provide an array of supplies the children can use to create their own panel. Consider the following:

1. Watercolors

2. Pastels

3. Acrylic paints

4. Construction paper (Cut out shapes represented in the painting and use them to make a mixed-media version.

5. Get even more creative and include sequins, beads, etc. as another way to vary the media used.

The goal is for the children to emulate Lawrence's piece by paying close attention to the shapes and colors he uses in this painting. Help them to see how an individual figure in the painting is composed essentially of different shapes. Consider, for instance, the following detail from the lower left side of the painting.

The picture to the left is the figure of a child. At its most essential, the head is a brown oval, the dress is a yellow triangle, and the arm is a thick brown line. Point these elements out. The children can focus on one part of the picture at a time, breaking the figure down by shape and color, and re-creating what they see. They may need to work on this for more than one session. Because we provide a four-day plan, more time can be used for art on the fifth day when there is no new material for Literature, Bible or Latin.

Also consider allowing each child to create more than one version of this panel. For instance, a child might do one version all in watercolor and another in pastels to become familiar with what it's like to work with different materials.

See the Appendix for a step by step example.

BIBLE GROUP
WEEK 1 - LOVE

DAY ONE -

DISCUSS: Remind the students of today's virtue focus. Today's focus is **love**. Make a new memory card for each term with its meaning and its opposite on the back of the card. These can be used for memory matching games once there are enough of them. Identify themes that go with the story and write terms and definitions on flash cards.

Focus Virtue: Love is caring for a person or thing very much and wishing good towards them.

Vice: Hate is disliking a person or thing very much and wishing harm towards them.

READ: Read the story of Jonathan and David. Encourage narration activities as students listen (drawing, writing, etc.).

Bible Story: Jonathan and David
1 Samuel 18-20

Saul was the Israelites first king. He was a tall handsome man, and at first it seemed he would make a good king. But soon his pride got in the way and he disobeyed and disrespected Jehovah. Jehovah is a special name for God. Because of this, Jehovah decided that Saul would no longer be his chosen king over Israel. Instead, he picked a new king - a shepherd boy named David - who would grow up and become king after Saul. David began doing great things with Jehovah's help, including killing a terrible giant named Goliath who was attacking the people.

When Saul saw the great things David was doing, he realized that Jehovah was with David, and not with him. His heart filled with envy, anger, and hatred. But Saul's oldest son, Jonathan, loved and served Jehovah, and he and David had become best friends. The young men loved each other like true brothers, and Jonathan had even given his own royal robes to David.

Over time, Saul became so jealous of David, that he decided to kill him and he tried to convince Jonathan to go along with his plans. But Jonathan warned David to stay out of the palace, and then he went to his father to try and save David.

Jonathan pleaded, "Do not sin against your servant David, because he has not sinned against you, and because his actions have brought good to you. For by him Jehovah saved all of Israel. You saw it, and were happy. Why then will you sin by killing David for no reason?"

Saul said that he had been wrong - he would not kill David - and he told Jonathan to bring David back. David returned to the palace, where he served Saul as before. But some months later, while David was playing beautiful harp music, Saul picked up his spear and threw it at him, hoping to pin him to the wall! David ducked quickly and managed to escape from the palace.

After that, David asked Jonathan to meet him secretly. David cried out, "What have I done? Why does your father want to kill me?"

Surprised, Jonathan answered, "My father has told me nothing of this!"

"I am very sure," replied David, "There is an inch between me and death!" Jonathan began to pace up and down, his heart full of troubles.

"What do you want me to do?" asked Jonathan, "I will do whatever you ask."

"There is a feast tomorrow," said David, "and I would normally be there at the royal table. When your father asks where I am, tell him you gave me permission to go home for a while. If he is angry, then we will know he wants to kill me, but if he is happy, then I will know I may come back. Please tell me the truth. If I deserve to die for any wrong I have done to your father, kill me yourself."

"As I live," swore Jonathan, "if my father seeks to harm you, I will help you escape. May our God Jehovah be with you always. I know a day is coming when Jehovah will destroy all your enemies and make you king over his people. When that day comes, please let me serve you and please protect my family." And the two men took solemn promises to protect each other and their families forever, for Jonathan loved David as much as he loved himself.

At the feast, Saul asked Jonathan where David was. As he had promised, Jonathan told his father that he had given David permission to go home. Saul became furious and his face grew red.

"You have sided with David?!" shouted Saul, "You horrible son! Don't you know that while David lives, you will never be king?"

But Jonathan replied, "What has he done to deserve death?" At this Saul became so angry that he picked up his spear and threw it at his own son. Full of anger and sadness on behalf of his friend, Jonathan left the palace and travelled to the field where he had promised to meet David. There he told David that indeed his father sought his life. Both men shed tears, and Jonathan helped David leave the city so that he could be safe.

Many years later, David did become king. By that time, Jonathan had already lost his life in a battle with Israel's enemies, but David remembered his promise and sought out Jonathan's son and protected him always.

DISCUSS:

1. How does Jonathan show his love for David? How does David show his love for Jonathan?

2. Why does Saul hate David? What does he do with his hate? Does David deserve Saul's hate?

3. Have you ever tried to help someone you cared about?

MEMORIZE:

Have children read and practice saying the memory sentence.

Memory Sentence: Jonathan loved David more than he loved the chance to be king.

FOLLOW-UP ACTIVITIES:

1. DRESS UP

Have the children act out the story.

Suggested dress up items:

- Beautiful robe (Jonathan and David)

- Spear

- Chair (throne)

- Small harp (David)

- Toy guitar or ukulele to stand for harp

- Crown (Saul)

2. BRAINSTORM

Write the main persons, places and things from the story up on white board or paper with space beneath them. Brainstorm descriptive words to go under each OR have descriptive words written in advance on stickies for younger kids. In the case of younger children, call out each term and ask for student volunteer to put each term under the person, place, or thing that it describes. Keep this for the next session.

PEOPLE

- David - brave, loyal, honest, promise-keeping, friend, love by Jehovah, loving

- Saul - hateful, angry, jealous, envious, treacherous, hasty, vindictive, rash, violent

THINGS

- Spear - thrown, dangerous, deadly

3. DICTATION

Make into a game and earn gems based on accuracy.

Pre-K and Kindergarten

The pre-k exercises are provided on a worksheet. The worksheets are accessible through a digital link provided upon purchase.

- David - begins with S, M, D, or B

- Jonathan - begins with Q, P, B, or J

- Saul - begins with S, W, C, or L

- King - begins with A, K, T, or U

Elementary Level

Early and later elementary students should complete their dictation exercises in their individual notebooks. See the Appendix for more on the kind of notebooks to use.

Early Elementary

- Jonathan saved his friend David.

(For this more complex version of the sentence, it makes sense to write on the board the spelling for uncommon names like Demeter, Hades, and Persephone.)

Later Elementary

- Saul tried to kill David because he was jealous. Jonathan and David were friends. Jonathan protected David from his father's violence.

4. CLOSING GAMES

See Appendix. Opportunity for more games (e.g. number knockout; card matching game based on story; etc).

DAY TWO -

DISCUSS - Remind the students of today's virtue focus. Today's focus is love. Refer to memory cards for love and hate introduced in the first session. Encourage them to say the memory sentences aloud from memory.

Focus Virtue: Love is caring for a person or thing very much and wishing good towards them.

Vice: Hate is disliking a person or thing very much and wishing harm towards them.

READ - Read the story of Jesus Raises Lazarus. Encourage narration activities as students listen (drawing, writing, etc.).

Bible Story: Jesus Raises Lazarus

John 11-12, Matthew 26

A few short weeks before Jesus' death and resurrection, a messenger came to speak to Jesus. He told him the sad news that Jesus' friend Lazarus had died. Jesus set out for Bethany, the city where Lazarus lived. When they heard that Jesus had arrived, Martha, the sister of Lazarus, ran out to meet Jesus.

Her eyes were full of tears and she said, "Lord, if you had been here, my brother would not have died. Even now I know that whatever you ask from Jehovah, Jehovah will give to you."

Jesus answered, "Martha, your brother will rise up from the dead and be alive again."

Martha replied, "I know that he will rise again on the last day."

Jesus looked at her and said, "I am the resurrection and the life. Whoever believes in me, even if he dies, will live forever. Do you believe this?"

"Yes," she answered, "I believe that you are the Messiah, the son of Jehovah, who is coming into the world." And she ran to get her sister, Mary, who sat weeping in their home.

Jesus entered the village and Mary, with many other people, came to greet him. When Jesus saw their tears, he was very sad.

"Where have you laid him," he asked.

The people led him to Lazarus' tomb, which was a cave with a large stone covering the entrance. Standing outside the tomb, Jesus wept. And the people said to each other how much Jesus must have loved Lazarus.

But then Jesus looked up and said to Martha, "Have this stone removed."

She was very surprised. "Lord!" she said, "he has been in the tomb for four days now and he will stink!"

"I told you," Jesus replied, "If you believe, you will see the glory of Jehovah!" And so they removed the stone from the entrance to the cave.

Then Jesus prayed to Jehovah and said loudly, "Lazarus, come out!" And out walked Lazarus, alive and well! He was a bit tangled up in the cloths which they had wrapped his body with, so Jesus told the people to unwrap him.

Some of the Jewish leaders who witnessed this miracle became extremely angry. Now Jesus would be more popular than ever and people would listen to him instead of them. Secretly, they plotted to kill both Jesus and Lazarus.

Jesus had dinner soon after with Lazarus and his sisters Mary and Martha. How joyful they must have been, celebrating Lazarus' new life. While Martha served the food, Mary came in with a large bottle of extremely expensive perfume. She poured the perfume all over the head and the feet of Jesus, and then wiped his feet with her hair.

Judas Iscariot, one of Jesus' followers, was angry and he said, "Why did she do this? That perfume could have been sold and all that money given to the poor!" Judas did not really care about the poor. His job was to hold the money purse for Jesus and the disciples, and he was a greedy thief!

But Jesus said, "Leave her alone! It is a beautiful thing Mary has done for me. She has anointed me for my burial. From now and for always, when people tell of the good news, she will be remembered because she has done this. You will always have the poor with you but I am leaving very soon."

Then Judas went and found the Jewish leaders and asked how much they would give him if he agreed to betray Jesus. The Jewish leaders said that if he would help them arrest Jesus, they would give him 30 pieces of silver. Judas agreed and began to watch for an opportunity to betray him.

DISCUSS:

1. Who did Jesus love in this story? Who loved Jesus? How could you tell?

2. Why did Mary pour the perfume onto Jesus?

3. Why was Judas angry at Mary?

4. Did anyone demonstrate hate in this story? How?

MEMORIZE:

Memory Sentence: Jesus loved Lazarus and raised him from the dead.

FOLLOW-UP ACTIVITIES:

1. **DRESS UP -** For narration involving dress up here are some items to consider including in a dress up box:

Suggested dress up item

- sandals, robe (for Jesus)
- pretty bottle (for Mary)
- money bag (for Judas)
- plates/cups
- strips of white cloth (grave clothes

2. **BRAINSTORM**

Write main persons, places and things from the story up on white board or paper with space beneath them. Brainstorm descriptive words to go under each. OR have descriptive words written in advance on stickies for younger kids. Call them out and ask volunteers to put each term under the person, place or thing that it describes. Keep this for the next session.

People

- Jesus - compassionate, grieved, resurrecting, weeping, comforting
- Lazarus - dead, raised, joyful, friend, brother
- Martha - sad, grieved, heartbroken, hopeful, loving, generous, lavish, sister
- Judas - thief, traitor, angry, selfish, resentful

Place

- Bethany - home to Lazarus, Mary, and Martha, village
- Tomb - dark, sealed, full, opened, empty

Things

- Perfume - expensive, nice smelling, anointing, poured out

3. DICTATION - This can be done by students individually or you can make it into a game where they earn gems based on accuracy.

Make into a game and earn gems based on accuracy.

Pre-K and Kindergarten

The pre-k exercises are provided on a worksheet. The worksheets are accessible through a digital link provided upon purchase.

- Lazarus - begins with Z, L, B, or U
- Mary - begins with M, E, S, or P.
- Tomb - begins with K, R, T, or M.
- Perfume - begins with A, R, D, or P.

Elementary Level

Early and later elementary students should complete their dictation exercises in their individual notebooks. See the Appendix for more on the kind of notebooks to use.

Early Elementary

- Jesus raised Lazarus from the dead.

Later Elementary

- Jesus raised Lazarus from the dead. Mary anointed Jesus with special perfume. Judas was angry and planned to betray Jesus.

4. CLOSING GAMES - Opportunities to earn more gems

- Number Knockout
- Card Matching Game based on story; etc.).

DAY THREE -

DISCUSS - Remind the students of today's virtue focus. Today's focus is love. Review memory sentences for love and hate.

> **Focus Virtue:** Love is caring for a person or thing very much and wishing good towards them.

> **Vice:** Hate is disliking a person or thing very much and wishing harm towards them.

READ - Introduce Lt. John Fox and Amy Carmichael. Tell their stories, introduce their memory sentences, and discuss their lives. Encourage narration activities as students listen (drawing, writing, etc.).

Historical Persons: John Fox and Amy Carmichael

John Fox was born in the state of Ohio in 1915. After attending college, he joined the army's officer training corps and graduated as a second lieutenant in 1940. The following year, America entered World War II, and John Fox was sent overseas. In December of 1944, John Fox was fighting German soldiers in Italy with the rest of his division. The Germans were attacking a town, and Fox was in a tall building helping direct airstrikes against advancing German troops in the town. But the Germans were soon gathered directly around the building where Fox sat. Immediately, he called in his own location as the best place to send the next volley of strikes. The radio operator asked him if he had made a mistake - he had called down an air strike on his own head! But Fox said to fire anyway. Fox died in that next volley, but the airstrike stopped the Germans from advancing and allowed Fox's fellow soldiers time to regroup and attack back. In 1997, Fox was given the Medal of Honor for his bravery and selfless sacrifice for the soldiers he protected and the country he loved.

MEMORIZE:

Memory Sentence: Lt. Fox loved his fellow soldiers and his country more than his own life.

Photo Credit: https://www.evangelical-times.org/40214/
the-life-and-legacy-of-amy-carmichael/#event-i-h-newman

Amy Carmichael was born in Ireland in 1867, the oldest of seven children. She served as a Christian missionary to India for many years. At that time, Indian families were expected to provide dowries, which are large sums of money, in order for their daughters to get married. Many families could not afford this, and other families simply wanted the gods to bless them, so some Indian families would sell their daughters as slaves to local Hindu temples. Amy began rescuing children from this horrible slavery.

Preena was the first little girl Amy rescued. She had tried to run away from the temple before and been cruelly treated when they caught her. But then she heard Amy talking about Jesus in the streets and she followed her. Amy provided a home and safety for Preena and eventually hundreds of other girls just like her. Despite the danger, Amy would sometimes rescue the girls by sneaking them out of the temples. The girls called her "Amma", which means mother. When asked why they went to Amy, they said it was because they knew that she loved them. Over the fifty years she lived in India, Amy also fought hard to get the laws changed to better protect children from slavery. Amy died surrounded by the girls she had rescued in 1951.

MEMORIZE:

Memory Sentence: Amy loved and rescued girls in India.

FOLLOW-UP ACTIVITIES:

1. **DICTATION -** Dictation based on simplified life story of historical figures. Once the students are finished, put the correct version up on the wall or board and have children make corrections. Discuss areas of uncertainty or confusion so students understand how to correct mistakes and understand why they were wrong. Make into a game or opportunity for earning gems based on accuracy.

   Pre - K

   - John - begins with an M, R, K, or J
   - Fox - begins with O, F, B, or K
   - Amy - begins with a U, A, M, or E
   - Carmichael - begins with a C, Y, N, or Q

Early Elementary

- John Fox saved his fellow soldiers in World War II.

- Amy Carmichael rescued girls from slavery in India.

Later Elementary

- John Fox served in the army during WWII. He sacrificed his own life to help the other soldiers beat the German army.

- Amy Carmichael served as a missionary in India. She rescued girls from slavery and brought them up as her own children.

2. CLOSING GAMES

See Appendix. Opportunity for more games. (e.g. number knockout; card matching game based on story; etc.).

DAY FOUR -

LEARNING THROUGH ART: See Learning Through Art, Week 1 for instructions.

OPTIONAL PICTURE STUDY - Use the photo above. Have the students look at the picture for 2 minutes.

Photo credit: https://christianhistoryinstitute.org/magazine/article/haystacks-%20starry-clusters-and-baptizing-bishops

Discussion Questions:

1. Compare this photo of Amy Carmichael and the one from the lesson from when she was much younger. What do you notice?

2. What is Amy wearing in the earlier photo? What is she wearing now?

3. What is Amy holding on her lap in each photo?

LATIN/SKILLS GROUP

WEEK 1 -
THE DOGS AND
THE FOX

DAY ONE -

DISCUSS - Before starting this activity; create cards with the Latin words in the vocabulary ban for this story. You will find these highlighted in the box below. Create a set of one-sided cards with only the Latin terms; another set of one-sided cards with their English meanings; and a third set of cards with the latin on front and the English on back. This will allow for different kinds of games and review. Introduce and discuss the vocabulary words before reading the fable.

VOCABULARY	
Canes - Dog (Canine)	**Clamat** - Shout (clamor)
Leonem - Lion (Leo the constellation)	**Fortes** - strong (fortitude)
Veterem/ Veteres - Old (veteran)	**Mementotes** - Remember (memento)
Vulpis - Fox	**Victus** - Loser (victim)

READ - "The Dogs and the Fox" in English.

THE DOGS AND THE FOX

Some dogs found the skin of a lion and furiously began to tear it with their teeth. A fox chanced to see them and laughed scornfully.

"If that Lion had been alive," he said, "it would have been a very different story. He would have made you feel how sharper his claws are then your teeth."

DISCUSS - Discuss the story using the discussion questions in the guide and/or questions you come up with.

Discussion Questions:

1. What is the message or lesson that you think this fable was trying to tell?

2. What do you think the fox was trying to tell the dogs?

3. What do you think this story is trying to teach?

4. Do you think this story has anything to do with love and hate? If so, what?

MEMORIZE - Memorize the Latin words from the vocabulary bank using one of the review methods below:

- When working with younger children who are not yet reading fluently (4-6), tell them the Latin word, show it to them, and then ask them to create an action, facial expression, or motion to show them a Latin card. Say the word and their task with the action, expression, or motion they agreed on. As they get the hang of it, go faster and faster. This helps them to associate the correct English meaning to each corresponding Latin term.

- Younger children will also enjoy the game, "Canis, Canis, Lupus". This is played by the same rules as "Duck, Duck, Goose". Canis is Latin for dog and Lupus is Latin for wolf. Since they haven't yet been introduced to the word "lupus", substitute "vulpis" – the word for fox– which is part of today's story.

- When working with older elementary aged children who can read, you can play a card matching game by dividing the students into teams. Feel free to go through several rounds to help them ingrain the words in their memories. Older children (7-11) may also enjoy the more embodied approach described above for younger children.

- The activity Roman Fables in Action is also a good one for both younger and older children. Details for this are in the Appendix.

DAY TWO -

DISCUSS

- Ask the children to tell you what they remember from story "The Dogs and the Fox".

- Ask them to put the moral or lesson of the story in their own words. Have the group agree on what this is. Write this down and keep it for future sessions.

- Next, ask the children to help re-write the story in their own words. They should write down what they say, reading it back to them and asking them to help you get the wording right. Write the final summary down and keep it for future sessions.

- Next, tell them that they have all the information they need now to remember and teach the story to someone else. They will do this by memorizing and saying the following:

Canes et Vulpis

The Dogs and the Fox

The story goes that/ One day _____ (insert 2-3 sentence summary they came up with).

The moral is: _____ (insert the moral they came up with)

MEMORIZE - Memorize the poem in English. If you're ambitious, you can try to memorize the Latin version, too!

English:

Dogs come upon an old Lion, tear him apart.
Along comes Fox who shouts:
"Were that Lion young and strong,
You would not have been so bold.
And remember this, before too long,
You, like this Lion, will one day be old!"

Moral: Don't kick someone while they're down.

Latin:

Canēs Leōnem veterem inveniunt et dilaniant.

Vulpis forte advenit et ad Cānes **clamat**:

"Sī **Leō** iuvenis esset,

nōn tam **fortēs** essētis.

Et **memintotes** hōc, vōs quoque

Mōx **veterēs** eritis!

Praeceptum: Nolī oppugnāre aliquem quī iam **victus** est.

FOLLOW-UP ACTIVITIES:

1.   LATIN GAMES: Play some of the Latin games from the Appendix.

2.   MATH REVIEW GAMES: For children able to do arithmetic, play number knockout. *See the Appendix for more on the Number Knockout game.* For younger children, have them choose a number card and then place the correct number of counters by the number. Or, have younger children review number flash cards as high as they can go. Children can be divided into teams for any of these review games.

3.   LANGUAGE ARTS REVIEW GAMES: For younger children, divide into teams to identify letter flash cards. Each time a team member gets a card correct the team gets a point. For older children, play spelling bee. Divide into two teams in front of a chalk or white board. Call out the word and whoever spells it faster and correctly gets a point for their team.

DAY THREE -

DISCUSS - If you did not complete the moral and story re-telling for "The Dogs and the Fox" in your last session, start out by completing it now.

Next, tell them that they have all the information they need now to remember and teach the story to someone else. They will do this by memorizing and saying the following:

> Canes et Vulpis   -   The Dogs and the Fox

> The story goes that/ One day _____
> (insert the 2-3 sentence summary they came up with).
> The moral is: _____
> (insert the moral they cam up with)

If you did complete it last session, start out by reminding them of the moral and story re-telling they came up with last time and ask them to retell it using the formula above.

MEMORIZE -

English:

Dogs come upon an old Lion, tear him apart.
Along comes Fox who shouts:
"Were that Lion young and strong,
You would not have been so bold.
And remember this, before too long,
You, like this Lion, will one day be old!"

Moral: Don't kick someone while they're down.

Latin:

Canēs Leōnem veterem inveniunt et dilaniant.

Vulpis forte advenit et ad Cānes **clamat**:

"Sī **Leō** iuvenis esset,

nōn tam **fortēs** essētis.

Et **memintotes** hōc, vōs quoque

Mōx **veterēs** eritis!"

Praeceptum: Nolī oppugnāre aliquem quī iam **victus** est.

FOLLOW-UP ACTIVITIES:

1. **LATIN REVIEW GAMES:** Begin by reviewing all the Latin vocabulary cards you have made so far in a manner appropriate to the age of your students. Then, play some of the games from the Latin Teacher's Guide Appendix.

2. **MATH REVIEW GAMES:** For children able to do arithmetic, play number knockout. For younger children, have them choose a number card and then place the correct number of counters by the number. Or, have younger children review number flashcards as high as they can go. Children can be divided into teams for any of these review games.

3. **LANGUAGE ARTS REVIEW GAMES:** For younger children, divide into teams to identify letter flash cards. Each time a team member gets a card correct the team gets a point. For older children, play spelling bee. Divide into two teams in front of a chalk or white board. Call out the word and whoever spells it fastest and correctly gets a point for their team.

DAY FOUR -

LEARNING THROUGH ART: See Learning Through Art Week 1 for instructions.

APPENDIX

NOTEBOOKS FOR WRITING AND DRAWING DURING DICTATION AND NARRATION

Each child should have a small notebook or workbook for drawing and writing activities. We recommend using Nyansa's Year One Workbooks, see the example in the picture given on the right. If you do not purchase a workbook, we recommend the other notebook pictured on the right. You can find the notebooks featured at https://www.waldorfsupplies.com/shop/journals/

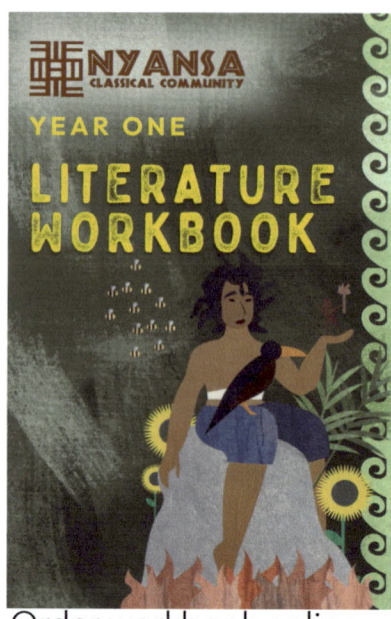

Order workbook online.

This notebook comes in several different colors, in 8x10 inches, and has pages that alternate every other page blank and every other page lined. So, for instance, when the child opens the notebook, the left side is blank and the right side is lined. If not this specific notebook, then find or create some other kind that has she same structure.

This kind of notebook is preferred for narration activities. While listening to the story, the child is encouraged to draw something of what she hears. For children who are able to write, the lined side can be used to write their own poem, narrative summary, or personal reflections on the story.

Lined page on the left and blank page on the right. This is how the entire notebook is structured. During a narration activity, the student can draw something from the story they are hearing on the blank side. If they are able to write, they can describe their picture on the left side.

Keeping such a notebook provides the following benefits:

- It provides a ready-made review of all the stories and ideas the child has engaged with.

- It allows the child, parents, and instructors to see progress over time throughout a single school year, and over several school years as this practice continues.

- It is a treasure in itself for the student. Family and instructor to simply enjoy the artwork, poetry, and writing produced by the student.

A lower elementary picture and summary based on read aloud from the *Odyssey*.

ART PROJECT SAMPLE

The photos and captions provide guidance on how to move from studying the image of an art work, to helping students imitate or create their own version of the art work. Here we are working with Panel 1 of Jacob Lawrence's famous Migration series.

Gather materials the children can use. Place the focal image on the table with the materials.

The student featured decided to use acrylic paint to re-create Lawrence's work. The paper is mixed-media paper which is strong and will take paint, glue, and other materials easily.

Next, she creates the place names and glues them over the trellis she painted. Materials: purple construction paper; white paint pen; brown acrylic paint; mixed media paper.

She decided to use her imagination to create new place names, reflecting places she would like to travel to. She will continue to work on the project on another day. This work took approximately 30-40 minutes to conceive and complete.

Process for more complex art project based on the same art work featured as well.

We decided to use varied materials, layering some on top of others, so first we cut out shapes and sizes we needed to create various parts of the art work. Materials used: blue tissue paper; brown construction paper; red construction paper, gold paint to write place names.

Next, we pasted blue tissue paper on the top half, then pasted brown bars on top of it.

Brown bars are cut into smaller pieces and glued to create lattice work. Next we add the signs with place names. Once the lattice is completed, we will use acrylic paint to paint the figures. This will be done on another day. Here you see the original art work juxtaposed with the new project in progress. It took approximately 30-40 minutes to complete this work.

See more pictures on the next page.

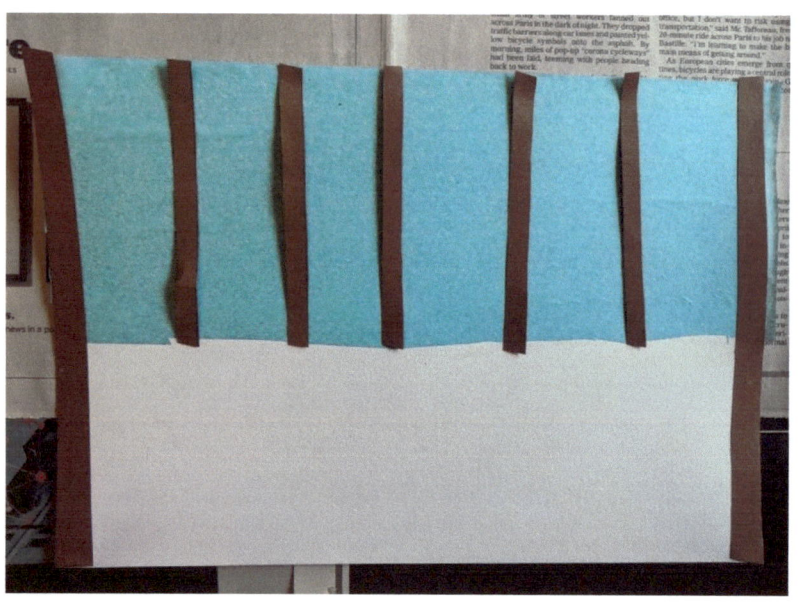

GAMES

NUMBER KNOCKOUT

Number Knockout is an exciting game that our children love to play. At the same time, it allows them to sharpen their numeracy skills. Type in the following link to go the National Number Knockout Site where you can see the basic rules, watch a demonstration video, and print out a game card:

YouTube link for a video of the game:

https://www.youtube.com/watch?v=u0krp-Q3l4U

PDF instructions:

https://thinksquare.com.au/wp-content/uploads/2016/04/Number-Knockout.pdf

This can easily be adapted to very young children who can do addition and subtraction. The board itself may be adapted for your children so that the number choices are very simple, small numbers.

We play this with individual children competing, or competing in teams and the children have lots of fun with it.

Enjoy!

LATIN GAMES

Flash cards mentioned in the games will be included in the full copy of materials.)

Roman Fables in Action (All Ages)

- Prep Time: <5 minutes
- Materials: Latin vocabulary cards
- Game Time: 10-20 minutes

Use the Latin vocabulary cards and sort them into separate decks (nouns/ verbs/ adjectives/ places).

1. Separate the students into groups (the size may depend on total students present and their age range, but usually 3-4 per group).

2. Give each group a card from each deck and have them create a scene to act out using the given noun, verb, adjective, and place. Have each group come up to act out their scene.

3. While a group performs, have the rest of the students guess the place, thing, adjective, and/or place in the scene. Depending on age and Latin proficiency, the students can guess using either the Latin or the English word.

4. After the scene has been correctly identified, the children who performed the scene will each read their Latin term aloud. Other students may be encouraged to repeat it.

5. Repeat until each group performs at least once.

Canis, Canis Lupus (Ages 4-8)

- Prep Time: None
- Materials: None
- Game Time: 10-15 minutes

1. Have the stunts sit in a circle.

2. Ask the group what two animals they would like to use to play this round. Encourage them to share what Latin animals they already know and can use! In this explanation, we will use Canis (dog) and Lupus (wolf).

3. One student at a time will walk around the circle tapping heads, saying "Canis" until they pick somebody at Lupus.

4. The Lupus will then get up and chase the first child around the circle until they sit back down at the original spot. Then the game repeats with Lupus being the new chooser.

Every few turns, you can encourage the children to change the animal terms. Supply new animal terms from the card deck if they are unfamiliar with them. The goal is for them to reinforce their current knowledge of the terms and to learn new ones!

Find a Latin Word that Classmates Describe (All Ages)

- Prep Time: None
- Materials: Latin vocabulary cards.
- Game Time (10-15 minutes (or until all students have had a turn to guess)

1. Have the students sit in a half circle or line.

2. Pick the first student in the line and pull them aside.

3. Show the remaining students a vocabulary card (the instructor can choose whether to show the English or Latin word), and tell them to think of ways to describe the word on the card without saying the actual word.

4. Have the student that has not been shown the card stand in front of their classmates and try to guess the Latin word that the other students were shown based off of their descriptions.

5. After the word is revealed, go through the rest of the students, make sure each one has a chance to guess a word.

Flyswatter (All Ages)

- Prep Time: <5 minutes
- Materials: Vocabulary cards (Latin side or English side)
- Game Time: 5-15 minutes

1. Before or after reading a fable, place the vocabulary cards from that fable on a table or other flat surface. The cards can be Latin-side up or English/Emoji-side up, depending on the method of play. Here are three possible methods:

A. **Latin-Side Up** - Say a vocabulary word in Latin, and have the students search the table for that card. Whoever slaps the card first wins that round.

B. **English-Side Up** - Say a vocabulary word in Latin and have the students slap the English translation. You can even do this while reading the fable: when you get to one of the words, say it emphatically to let the students know it's one of the words on the table. This will help them pay attention to the fable and draw on their own store of Latin words.

C. **Latin-Side Up** - For harder gameplay, say a vocabulary word in English and have the students slap the Latin word. This is great for older students, students that know Latin well, or for vocabulary that appears in many fables. If they can't come up with the word, encourage them to work together, give them a letter or two from the start of the word, or act out/mimic the word to jumpstart their thinking.

Latin Charades (All Ages)

- Prep Time: 5-10 minutes
- Materials: Latin vocabulary cards
- Game Time: 15-20 minutes

1. Use Latin vocabulary cards created from each lesson, and sort them into decks (nouns/ verbs/ adjectives/ places).

2. Choose a deck and have the students all gather in a circle.

3. Have one student at a time come to the front, give them a card from the deck, and have them act it out. If it is a noun deck, they should act like the animal/ person on the card. If it is a verb deck, they should perform the action on the card.

4. The first student to correctly guess the word earns a point. There is room for modification with various levels of Latin proficiency. For an older group, they might have to say the Latin term to get the point. For another group, the English term may be sufficient.

5. After the word has been correctly guessed, the child who performed charades will read the Latin term aloud. Encourage the others to repeat it back!

6. Repeat until each student has had a chance to perform a word.

Simius Says (All Ages)

- Prep Time: None
- Materials: Latin vocabulary cards (optional)
- Game Time: 5-15 minutes

1. Have the students stand in a line or in rows (depending on class size).

2. As Simius the Monkey Judge, give commands from the Latin vocabulary cards. If the card is an animal or person, the students should act like them (for example, if the word is "Rana", they should get down and hop like a frog.) If the card is a verb, they should perform the action the verb describes (such as turning if they hear "verto/vertere"). Many of the actions in the charades game should also work well here. For extra clarity, perform these actions yourself if the desired action is unclear to the students.

3. Be sure to say "Simius Says" before giving a command. If the command does not start this way, then the students should not follow the command.

4. If a student does not follow the commands or performs them incorrectly, then Simius rules them out.

5. Play continues until one student remains. If time allows, they can become the next Monkey Judge.

6. For a more advanced form of this game, use the imperative forms of the verb cards (for example, "vertite!" would be telling the students to turn). You can even differentiate between singular and plural imperatives as a means of eliminating the students (if they perform an action that is command in the singular, rule them out). This works especially well for teaching older groups of students about Latin imperatives.

Tossed Speech (Best Suited for Younger Ages)

- Prep Time: None
- Materials: Throwing ball
- Game Time: 5-15 minutes

1. Have students stand in a circle.

2. Have the students toss a ball from one student to another.

3. Each time a student catches a ball, they must say a Latin vocabulary word (you can pick a theme such as animals, verbs, or places, or let the students pick for themselves).

4. Upon hearing the word, the rest of the students repeat it and then translate it.

5. The first student throws the ball to another student.

6. This process repeats until the students run out of words. If the students do this activity after reading a fable, it may help them internalize the vocabulary. Telling them about the activity beforehand will also make sure they pay attention during the reading.

7. For easier gameplay, the students could pick vocabulary cards before the game starts to they have Latin words in mind.

8. For more difficult gameplay, have the students repeat each word that has already been said after another is added. For example, if the first student says "canis", the second will say "leo, canis", and the third "felis, leo, canis", and so on. This is a great test of students' attention spans, as the lists may get quite long after several turns!

Trans, Iter, Sub, Super

- Prep Time: 3-5 minutes
- Materials: None
- Game Time: 5-10 minutes

1. Write the instructions for the gestures on a board or post instructions in the classroom.

2. Teach the students the following song, to the tune of "Heads, Shoulders, Knees and Toes" (Sing it a few times if you want to make sure.):

    "Trans, Inter, Sub, Super, Sub, Super (x2)
    In, et ad, et ab, ex, per
    Trans, Inter, Sub, Super, Sub, Super, Circus!"

3. Teach the children the following gestures to do while singing:

Trans - Move your right hand across your chest diagonally

Inter - Place the palms of your hands on each side of your head

Sub - Move your head down, while lifting your shoulders

Super - Stand up and move your arms up above your head

In - Hug yourself

Et ad - Take one step forward

Et ab - Take one step backward

Ex - Point to the door or exit

Per - Clasp your hands together and move them forward

Circum - Spin in a circle

Verba Cum Amicis/ Words With Friends (All Ages)

- Prep Time: None

- Materials: Scrabble board and letter tiles

- Game Time: 5-10 minutes

    Using a Scrabble board and letter tile (or whatever similar materials may be available), encourage students to spell Latin vocabulary that they are familiar with. Alternatively, have them read Latin words that you and other students have made out of the tiles. Seeing the words spelled out may help them to recognize some of the ways in which Latin differs from English (such as the letter "V" being pronounced like a "W" or the letter "I" often replacing the letter "J").

1. Once a word is formed, read, or understood, allow the students to act out this new word (such as walking on all fours and barking like a canis, or dog).

www.ingramcontent.com/pod-product-compliance
Lightning Source LLC
Chambersburg PA
CBHW040813120626

46547CB00004B/539